An Annotated Bibliography of Smollett Scholarship

1946-68

An Annotated Bibliography of Smollett Scholarship
1946-68

DONALD M. KORTE

University of Toronto Press

Printed in Canada

SBN 8020-1676-6

Contents

Preface

This bibliography has been compiled to aid Smollett scholars locate the numerous books, doctoral dissertations, articles, and notes written about Smollett in recent years. The year 1946 was taken as a starting point because this bibliography is intended to supplement Francesco Cordasco's *Smollett Criticism, 1925-1945: A Compilation* (Brooklyn, 1947). All items thought to be of interest to Smollett scholars have been cited. Editions of Smollett's writings containing critical commentary as well as noteworthy general introductions to Smollett appearing in histories of the novel have been included. Only queries which provide no information on Smollett and reprints of works published before 1946 have been omitted. The large number of items for the relatively short period of twenty-three years indicates the academic world's continuing interest in Tobias Smollett.

The information for each entry is as complete as circumstances would allow: several dissertations are not annotated because it was impossible to examine these works or because no abstract was available. A word of caution: a few 1968 dissertations may not have been listed. This situation exists because of the time lag that occurs between the completion of a dissertation and its citation in *Dissertation Abstracts.* The only way to have avoided possible omissions of 1968 dissertations would have been to delay publication of this bibliography for at least another year.

I would like to thank the Canada Council and the University of Guelph for their assistance in this project.

D. M. K.

Guelph, Ontario
July 1969

An Annotated Bibliography of Smollett Scholarship

Bibliography

1946

1
Heilman, Robert B. "Falstaff and Smollett's Micklewhimmen" *Review of English Studies,* XXII (1946), 226-8

Falstaff is a likely source for Micklewhimmen, a character in *Humphry Clinker.*

2
J., C. E. "Smollett's *Peregrine Pickle:* a Note" *Notes and Queries,* CXC (1946), 213

Reprints a letter written by Daniel MacKercher, who refutes the idea that he is the Mr. M – in Volume IV of *Peregrine Pickle.*

3
McCullough, Bruce W. *Representative English Novelists: Defoe to Conrad* New York: Harper and Row, 1946 Pp. ix + 359

Roderick Random is discussed in Chapter IV, "The Picaresque Novel," pp. 58-68.

4
Norwood, L. F. "Imposition of a Half-Sheet in Duodecimo" *Library,* 5th series, I (1946), 242-4

Concerns the first edition of *Humphry Clinker.*

5
Pritchett, Victor S. *The Living Novel*
London: Chatto & Windus, 1946 Pp. xi + 260

See "The Shocking Surgeon," pp. 18-23.

6
Putney, Rufus "Smollett and Lady Vane's Memoirs" *Philological Quarterly,* xxv (1946), 120-6

Asserts that Smollett had a hand in the composition of the "Memoirs," which appear in *Peregrine Pickle.*

7
Young, Percy M. "Observations on Music by Tobias Smollett" *Music & Letters,* xxvii (1946), 18-24

Discusses references to music and musicians in Smollett's novels and in his other works.

1947

8
Boege, Fred W. *Smollett's Reputation as a Novelist*
Princeton: Princeton University Press, 1947 Pp. 175

Reviews
L. M. Knapp, *Journal of English and Germanic Philology,* xlvii, 98-100
J. M. S. Tompkins, *Review of English Studies,* xxiv, 373-4
Louis L. Martz, *Modern Language Notes,* lxiii, 565-6

Traces the uneven course of Smollett's literary reputation from 1748 to 1940 by citing reactions to Smollett both in Europe and in America.

9
Cordasco, Francesco *Smollett Criticism, 1925-1945: a Compilation*
Brooklyn: Long Island University Press, 1947 Pp. vi + 9

A list of 73 items – some with annotations.

10
Mack, Edward C. "Pamela's Stepdaughters: The Heroines of Smollett and Fielding" *College English,* VIII (1947), 293-301

Describes the model heroine of the eighteenth century and argues that Smollett's leading ladies do not deviate from this norm.

11
Oppenheimer, Jane M. "A Note on William Hunter and Tobias Smollett" *Journal of the History of Medicine,* II (1947), 481-6

About Smollett's friendship with William Hunter, physician.

1948

12
Cordasco, Francesco "The Ascription of 'A Sorrowful Ditty ...' to Smollett Affirmed" *Notes and Queries,* CXCIII (1948), 428-9

13
Cordasco, Francesco "J. P. Browne's Edition of Smollett's Works" *Notes and Queries,* CXCIII (1948), 428-9

14
Cordasco, Francesco "A *Peregrine Pickle* Play, 1929" *Notes and Queries,* CXCIII (1948), 142-3

Discusses a play presented in 1929 by Kate Parsons entitled "The Commodore Marries," which is based on *Peregrine Pickle.*

15
Cordasco, Francesco "Robert Anderson's Edition of Smollett" *Notes and Queries,* CXCIII (1948), 533

16
Cordasco, Francesco "Smollett's Creditor Macleane Identified" *Notes and Queries,* CXCIII (1948), 141-2

17
Cordasco, Francesco *Smollett Criticism, 1770-1924: a Bibliography, Enumerative and Annotative*
Brooklyn: Long Island University Press, 1948 Pp. iv + 28

Cites 305 items.

18
Cordasco, Francesco "Smollett and His Detractor, Hugh Blair: with an Unpublished Smollett Letter" *Notes and Queries,* CXCIII (1948), 295-6

19
Cordasco, Francesco "Smollett and Petronius" *Modern Language Quarterly,* IX (1948), 415-17

Discusses the influence of Petronius' *Satyricon* upon Smollett's work.

20
Cordasco, Francesco "Smollett and the Translation of the *Don Quixote* – a Critical Bibliography" *Notes and Queries,* CXCIII (1948), 383-4

Lists 18 items.

21
Cordasco, Francesco "Smollett and the Translation of the *Don Quixote:* Important Unpublished Letters" *Notes and Queries,* CXCIII (1948), 363-4

22
Cordasco, Francesco "Smollett and the Translation of Fénelon's *Telemachus*" *Notes and Queries,* CXCIII (1948), 563

Rejects the claim that Smollett translated *Telemachus.*

23
Deutsch, Otto E. "Poetry Preserved in Music: Bibliographical Notes on Smollett and Oswald, Handel, and Haydn" *Modern Language Notes,* LXIII (1948), 73-88

Provides Smollett's lyrics to a song and to his "Alceste."

24
Kline, Judd "Three Doctors and Smollett's Lady of Quality" *Philological Quarterly,* XXVII (1948), 219-28

Discusses the identity of "Dr. S – ," who (according to Howard Buck) supervised the composition of Lady Vane's "Memoirs." Kline concludes that "Dr. S – " is Dr. Peter Shaw, not Smollett or Shebbeare.

25
Linsalata, Carmine "Tobias Smollett's Translation of 'Don Quixote'" *Library Chronicle of the University of Texas,* III (1948), 55-68

Attempts to prove Smollett's debt to Charles Jarvis' translation of *Don Quixote.*

26
Moore, Robert E. *Hogarth's Literary Relationships*
London: Oxford University Press, 1948 Pp. viii + 202

Includes a chapter concerned with Smollett.

1949

27
Cordasco, Francesco "Smollett and the Death of King William III" *Modern Language Notes,* LXIV (1949), 21-3

Concerns the source of an anecdote which appears in Smollett's *Complete History of England.*

28
Cordasco, Francesco "Smollett's 'Register of the Weather'" *Notes and Queries,* CXCIV (1949), 163

Maintains that Smollett got the idea of appending "A Register of the Weather" to his *Travels Through France and Italy* (London, 1766) from contemporary magazines which often included such registers.

29
Cordasco, Francesco "Smollett and the Translation of the *Gil Blas*"
Modern Language Quarterly, X (1949), 68-71

30
Cordasco, Francesco "Two Notes on Smollett" *Notes and Queries,* CXCIV
(1949), 557-8

Describes a work written by Laughlin Macleane, Smollett's creditor; quotes a Smollett story from *Percy Anecdotes*; and identifies an individual who provided the model for Hugh Strap of *Roderick Random.*

31
Foster, James R. *History of the Pre-Romantic Novel in England*
London: Oxford University Press, 1949 Pp. xi + 294

See especially pp. 120-30

32
Graham, W. H. "Smollett's *Humphry Clinker*"
The Contemporary Review, CLXXVI (1949), 33-8

A general description of *Humphry Clinker.*

33
Green, David Bonnell "Keats and Smollett" *Notes and Queries,* CXCIV
(1949), 558-9

Allusions to *Humphry Clinker* in Keats' letters.

34
Knapp, Lewis M. "Smollett's Self-portrait in *The Expedition of Humphry Clinker*" *The Age of Johnson: Essays Presented to Chauncey Brewster Tinker,* ed. F. W. Hilles
New Haven: Yale University Press, 1949 Pp. 149-58

Examines the autobiographical dimension of *Humphry Clinker* and maintains that Bramble, Jerry Melford, and Lismahago offer Smollett media for self-revelation.

35
Knapp, Lewis M. *Tobias Smollett: Doctor of Men and Manners*
Princeton: Princeton University Press, 1949 Pp. xiii + 362

Reviews
James L. Clifford, *New York Times Book Review,* 30 January, p. 5
Times Literary Supplement, 26 August, p. 552
Robert E. Moore, *Journal of English and Germanic Philology,* XLIX, 118-20
Eugene Joliat, *University of Toronto Quarterly,* XXI, 103-4
J. M. S. Tompkins, *Review of English Studies,* n.s. II, 286-8

The standard biographical study of Smollett. Contains a chapter on Smollett's contribution to the English novel (pp. 309-24).

36
Oppenheimer, Jane M. "John and William Hunter and Some Contemporaries in Literature and Art" *Bulletin of the History of Medicine,* XXIII (1949), 21-47

Smollett is mentioned briefly as a friend of John and William Hunter, physicians.

37
Sherwood, Irma Z. "The Novelists as Commentators" *The Age of Johnson: Essays Presented to Chauncey Brewster Tinker,* ed. F. W. Hilles
New Haven: Yale University Press, 1949 Pp. 113-25

Smollett's practice of using his characters as a mouthpiece for his own sentiments is briefly discussed on pp. 118 and 121.

38
Smollett, Tobias *Roderick Random* With an afterword by R. Samarin
Moscow: 1949 Pp. 531-9

39
Smollett, Tobias *Travels Through France and Italy* Introduction by Osbert Sitwell
London: Lehmann, 1949 Pp. xiv + 303

40
Todd, William B. "The Number and Order of Certain Eighteenth-Century Editions" Dissertation, Chicago, 1949

See pp. 48-50, 131-5 for a discussion of the difficulty of establishing an accurate text of *Humphry Clinker.*

1950

41
Cordasco, Francesco, ed. *Letters of Tobias George Smollett: A Supplement to the Noyes Collection with a Bibliography of Editions of the Collected Works*
Madrid: Imp. Avelino Ortega, Cuesta de Sancti-Spiritus, 1950 Pp. 46

Contains 31 letters. For the controversy over the authenticity of five of these letters, see *Philological Quarterly,* XXX (1951), 290-1 and XXXI (1952), 299-300

42
Cordasco, Francesco "Smollett's German Medical Degree" *Modern Language Notes,* LXV (1950), 117-19

According to a letter signed by a Charles Fizès, Smollett received a degree from the University of Giessen.

43
Cordasco, Francesco "An Unrecorded Medical Translation by Smollett" *Notes and Queries,* CXCV (1950), 516

44
Linsalata, Carmine R. "Smollett's Indebtedness to Jarvis' Translation of *Don Quijote*" *Symposium,* IV (1950), 84-106

Concludes that Smollett depended heavily upon Charles Jarvis' translation of *Don Quijote* (1742) and suggests that Smollett did not know Spanish well enough to translate Cervantes.

45
Newman, Franklin B. "A Consideration of the Bibliographical Problems Connected with the First Edition of *Humphry Clinker*" *Papers of the Bibliographical Society of America,* XLIV (1950), 340-71

46
Orr, John "Did Smollett Know Spanish?" *Modern Language Review,* XLV (1950), 218

In short, yes, he did.

47
Randall, David "*Humphry Clinker*" *The New Colophon,* II (1950), 379-80

Raises bibliographical questions about the early editions of *Humphry Clinker.*

48
Risch, Dithmar "Smollett und Deutschland. Deutschlandbild und Aufnahme in Deutschland" Dissertation, Goettingen, 1950

49
Shoup, Louise "The Use of the Social Gathering as a Structural Device in the Novels of Richardson, Fielding, Smollett, and Sterne" Dissertation, Stanford, 1950

Examines the various functions (satiric, informational etc.) of the social gathering in Smollett's novels.

50
Smollett, Tobias *The Expedition of Humphry Clinker* Edited with an introduction by Robert Gorham Davis
New York: Holt, Rinehart and Winston, 1950 Pp. xxviii + 414

51
Smollett, Tobias *Selected Writings* Edited with an introduction by Arthur Calder-Marshall
London: Falcon Press, 1950 Pp. 86

1951

52
Brander, Laurence *Tobias Smollett*
London: Longmans, 1951 Pp. 36

Review
Times Literary Supplement, 9 March, p. 154

A general introduction to Smollett – the man and his writings. A selected bibliography is appended to the text.

53
Davis, Robert Gorham "The Sense of the Real in English Fiction" *Comparative Literature,* III (1951), 200-17

See p. 212 for a discussion of Smollett.

54
Foster, James R. "*Peregrine Pickle* and the *Memoirs of Count Grammont*" *Modern Language Notes,* LXVI (1951), 469-71

Conjectures that Smollett borrowed the fortune-telling ruse in *Peregrine Pickle* from Hamilton's *Memoirs of Count Grammont.*

55
Spector, Robert D. "Late Neo-Classical Taste" *Notes and Queries,* CXCVI (1951), 11-12

Concerns the level of literary criticism which appeared in the *Critical Review,* 1756-60.

56
Todd, William B. "Bibliography and the Editorial Problem in the Eighteenth Century" *Studies in Bibliography,* IV (1951), 41-55

Mentions the problems of editing *Humphry Clinker.* See p. 50.

1952

57
Bastian, John L. "Smollett's and Goldsmith's Histories and the Mid-Eighteenth Century Reaction to the Genre of History" Dissertation, Boston, 1952

Investigates such matters as the following: Smollett's reaction to the "new history" of the Enlightenment, the relationship between history and the novel, Smollett's debt to Hume, and the style Smollett employs in his historical writings.

58
Cordasco, Francesco "Smollett and Fizès" *Modern Language Notes,* LXVII (1952), 360

After further investigation, Cordasco finds that the "Fizès" letter is indeed a forgery.

59
Cordasco, Francesco "Smollett and the Translation of *Don Quixote*" *Modern Language Quarterly,* XIII (1952), 23-36

Provides evidence (a letter) that Smollett's translation of *Don Quixote* was largely someone else's work. But see Knapp, *Modern Language Quarterly,* XIV (1953), 228.

60
Kirchner, Gustav "Shaw's *Pygmalion* und Smollett's *Peregrine Pickle*" *Die Neueren Sprachen,* n.s. I (1952), 409-17

Maintains that an episode in *Peregrine Pickle* provided Shaw with the idea for *Pygmalion.*

61
Knapp, Lewis M. and Lillian de la Torre "Smollett and Fizès (?)" *Modern Language Notes,* LXVII (1952), 69-71

Questions the authenticity of the "Fizès" letter which Cordasco referred to (*Modern Language Notes,* LXV, 117-19).

62
Lancaster, H. C. "The Death of William III: a Correction" *Modern Language Notes,* LXVII (1952), 432

Rejects Cordasco's assertion (*Modern Language Notes,* LXIV [1949], 21-3) about the source of an anecdote in Smollett's *History of England.*

63
Prickitt, Henry B. "The Political Writings and Opinions of Tobias Smollett" Dissertation, Harvard, 1952

Examines Smollett's political views which appear in his novels, verse satires, poems, histories, and in various journals.

64
Todd, William B. "Texts and Pretexts" *Papers of the Bibliographical Society of America,* XLVI (1952), 164

Questions the textual accuracy of the Rinehart edition of *Humphry Clinker.* See Robert G. Davis' "Reply" on p. 165 of *Papers of the Bibliographical Society of America.*

1953

65
Almirall, Catherine L. "Smollett's 'Gothic': an Illustration" *Modern Language Notes,* LXVIII (1953), 408-10

Smollett is indebted to Congreve's *Mourning Bride* for Gothic elements in *Ferdinand Count Fathom.*

66
Crockett, Harold K. "The Picaresque Tradition in English Fiction to 1770: a Study of Popular Backgrounds, with Particular Attention to Fielding and Smollett" Dissertation, Illinois, 1953

Argues that Smollett is indebted to native, not foreign sources, for the picaresque elements in his work.

67
Foster, James R. "Smollett and the *Atom*" *Publications of the Modern Language Association,* LXVIII (1953), 1032-46

Attempts to prove that Smollett was the author of *The History and Adventures of an Atom* (1769).

68
Knapp, Lewis M. and Lillian de la Torre "Forged 'Smollett' Letter" *Modern Language Quarterly,* XIV (1953), 228

Repudiates Cordasco (see "Smollett and the Translation of the *Don Quixote,*" *Modern Language Quarterly,* XIII [1952], 23-36) by pointing out that his thesis is based on a letter which is a forgery.

69
Knapp, Lewis M. "Forged 'Smollett' Letters" *Notes and Queries,* CXCVIII (1953), 163

Observes that the "unpublished letters of Tobias Smollett" brought to light by Cordasco (*Notes and Queries,* CXCIII [1948], 295-6, 363-4) are forgeries.

70
Pritchett, V. S. *Books in General*
London: Chatto and Windus, 1953 Pp. viii + 258

See Chapter XIV, "The Unhappy Traveller," for a discussion of Smollett's *Travels Through France and Italy.*

71
Smollett, Tobias *The Expedition of Humphry Clinker* With an introduction by A. Elistratova
Moscow: 1953 Pp. 3-17

1954

72
Allen, Walter *The English Novel*
New York: E. P. Dutton, 1954 Pp. xxiv + 454

Smollett's novels discussed on pp. 62-72 and passim.

73
Foster, James R. "A Forgotten Noble Savage, Tsonnonthouan"
Modern Language Quarterly, XIV (1954), 348-59

Smollett may be the author of a review of *The Memoirs of the Life and Adventures of Tsonnonthouan* (1763), which appears in the *Critical Review*. To support his hypothesis, Foster notes that *Humphry Clinker* contains echoes of *Tsonnonthouan*.

74
Knapp, Lewis M. "Abridgements of Smollett for Children" *Notes and Queries*, n.s. I (1954), 475

Describes a 1776 children's edition of *Roderick Random*.

75
Smollett, Tobias *Humphry Clinker*. With an introduction by V. S. Pritchett
London: William Collins, 1954 Pp. 352

1955

76
Goldberg, Milton A. "The Novels of Tobias Smollett: Analysis in an Eighteenth-Century Mode" Dissertation, John Hopkins, 1955

77
Harder, Kelsie B. "Genealogical Satire in *Humphry Clinker*" *Notes and Queries*, n.s. II (1955), 441-3

Provides background on *Humphry Clinker* by briefly describing some of the genealogies "in which Scottish antiquarians indulged their egos ... "

78
Knapp, Lewis M. "Abridgements of Smollett for Children" *Notes and Queries,* n.s. II (1955), 80-1

The same note which appeared in *Notes and Queries,* n.s. I (1954), 475.

79
Knowles, Edwin B. "A Note on Smollett's *Don Quixote*" *Modern Language Quarterly,* XVI (1955), 29-31

Objects to Cordasco's conclusions about Smollett's translation of *Don Quixote* in *Modern Language Quarterly,* XIII (1952), 23-36

80
Macalpine, Ida and Richard A. Hunter "*Sir Launcelot Greaves*" Letter in *Times Literary Supplement,* 16 December, p. 761

Identifies William Battie's *A Treatise on Madness* as the source of a passage in *Sir Launcelot Greaves.*

81
Myers, Sylvia H. "Ideals, Actuality and Judgment in the Novels of Tobias Smollett" Dissertation, University of California, Berkeley, 1955

82
Ruth, Friedrich "Die Weltanschauung Tobias Smolletts" Dissertation, Heidelberg, 1955

83
Scott, William "Smollett, Dr. John Hill, and the Failure of *Peregrine Pickle*" *Notes and Queries,* n.s. II (1955), 389-92

Quotes various attacks upon Smollett written by Hill, a contemporary of Smollett and a literary rival.

84
Smollett, Tobias *Peregrine Pickle* With an introduction by A. Elistratova Moscow: 1955 Pp. 3-13

85
Spector, Robert D. "Eighteenth-Century Political Controversy and Linguistics" *Notes and Queries,* n.s. II (1955), 387-9

Concerns the linguistic awareness of Smollett and his political adversaries in *The Briton* and in *The North Briton.*

86
Spector, Robert D. "Further Attacks on the *Critical Review*" *Notes and Queries,* n.s. II (1955), 535

87
Spector, Robert D. "Smollett and Admiral Byng" *Notes and Queries,* n.s. II (1955), 66-7

Discusses Smollett's non-objective treatment of Admiral Byng in his *History of England.*

88
Strauss, Albrecht B. "Design in the Novels of Tobias Smollett" Dissertation, Harvard, 1955

Refutes the charge that Smollett's novels are structureless and contends that Smollett achieved "a measure of structural and thematic cohesion" in his work.

89
Wasserman, Earl R. "Smollett's Satire on the Hutchinsonians" *Modern Language Notes,* LXX (1955), 336-7

Identifies Sir Mungo Barebones (a character in *Ferdinand Count Fathom*) as the theologian John Hutchinson.

1956

90
Hudson, A. Edward A. and Arthur Herbert "James Lind: His Contributions to Shipboard Sanitation" *Journal of the History of Medicine,* XI (1956), 1-12

Alludes to Smollett's account of the hardships of life at sea in *Roderick Random.* See page 3.

91
Knapp, Lewis M. "Smollett's Letter to Samuel Mitchelson" *Notes and Queries,* n.s. III (1956), 262

92
Linsalata, Carmine *Smollett's Hoax: 'Don Quixote' in English*
Stanford: Stanford University Press, 1956 Pp. ix + 116

Reviews
L. M. Knapp, *Journal of English and Germanic Philology,* LVII, 553-5
R. B. Tate, *Notes and Queries,* n.s. IV, 368

Concludes that Smollett plagiarized from Jarvis, that he did not know enough Spanish to translate Cervantes, and that he relegated the task of translating the *Quixote* to his hack writers. Several appendixes list parallel passages from Cervantes, Jarvis, Smollett, and others.

93
Macalpine, Ida and Richard A. Hunter "Smollett's Reading in Psychiatry" *Modern Language Review,* LI (1956), 409-11

See note to item 80.

94
Macalpine, Ida and Richard A. Hunter "Tobias Smollett, M.D., and William Battie, M.D." *Journal of the History of Medicine,* XI (1956), 102-3

See note to item 80.

95
McKillop, Alan Dugald *The Early Masters of English Fiction*
Lawrence: University of Kansas Press, 1956 Pp. 233

See Chapter IV entitled "Tobias Smollett" (pp. 147-81).

96
Milic, Louis T. "Sterne and Smollett's *Travels*" *Notes and Queries*, n.s. III (1956), 80-1

Demonstrates that Sterne, in *A Sentimental Journey*, repeatedly parodies Smollett's *Travels Through France and Italy*.

1957

97
Humphreys, A. R. "Fielding and Smollett" *From Dryden to Johnson*, ed. Boris Ford
Harmondsworth: Penguin, 1957 Pp. 313-32

Briefly assesses Smollett's achievement as a novelist and compares him with Fielding.

98
Jones, Claude E. "Smollett Editions in Eighteenth-Century Britain" *Notes and Queries*, n.s. IV (1957), 252

99
Jones, Claude E. "Tobias Smollett (1721-1771) – The Doctor as Man of Letters" *Journal of the History of Medicine*, XII (1957), 337-48

A general introduction to Smollett from the viewpoint of the physician as novelist.

100
Knapp, Lewis M. "Smollett's Translation of *Don Quixote*: Data on Its Printing and Its Copyright" *Notes and Queries*, n.s. IV (1957), 543-4

101
Lettis, Richard Lincoln "A Study of Smollett's *Sir Launcelot Greaves*" Dissertation, Yale, 1957

Provides a critical evaluation of *Sir Launcelot Greaves,* relates the work to contemporary minor fiction, analyzes its components, and links it to Smollett's other novels. Lettis also supplies annotations to this novel.

102
Roper, Derek "Tobias Smollett and the Founders of His *Review*" *Call Number* (Library of the University of Oregon), XIX (1957), 4-9

Identifies the founders of the *Critical Review* as Thomas Francklin, Samuel Derrick, John Armstrong, and Patrick Murdoch.

103
Scott, William "Smollett's 'The Tears of Scotland' A Hitherto Unnoticed Printing and Some Comments on the Text" *Review of English Studies,* n.s. VIII (1957), 38-42

104
Sheinker, V. "Tobias Smollett's *Ferdinand Count Fathom*" *Uchenye Zapiski Leningradskogo Universiteta (Transactions of Leningrad University),* No. 234 (1957), 3-22

105
Sheinker, V. "Tobias Smollett's *Roderick Random*" *Uchenye Zapiski Murmanskogo Pedinstituta (Transactions of the Murmansk Pedagogical College),* I (1957), 23-62

106
Taylor, Archer "Proverbial Materials in Tobias Smollett, *The Adventures of Sir Launcelot Greaves*" *Southern Folklore Quarterly,* XXI (1957), 85-92

Lists proverbs, proverbial phrases, and proverbial comparisons in *Sir Launcelot Greaves.*

1958

107
Cordasco, Francesco "Smollett in Dutch" *Notes and Queries,* n.s. v (1958), 181

A query concerning a Smollett work listed in a Dutch antiquarian's catalogue.

108
Dooley, D. J. "Some Uses and Mutations of the Picaresque" *Dalhousie Review,* XXXVII (1958), 363-77

See especially pp. 367-9 for a discussion of Smollett.

109
Jones, Claude E. "The English Novel: a *Critical* View (1756-1785)" *Modern Language Quarterly,* XIX (1958), 147-59, 213-24

Discusses criticism of the novel which appeared in the *Critical Review.*

110
Noyes, Robert Gale *The Neglected Muse: Restoration and Eighteenth-Century Tragedy in the Novel (1740-1780)*
Providence: Brown University Press, 1958 Pp. 187

Notes a few references to Thomas Otway, David Garrick, and James Quin in Smollett's novels. See especially pp. 99-101.

111
Orowitz, Milton "Smollett and the Art of Caricature" *Spectrum,* II (1958), 155-67

Analyzes Smollett's use of caricature and the philosophical implications of this technique.

112
Sheinker, V. "*Peregrine Pickle* and Some Features of Smollett's Satire" *Uchenye Zapiski Murmanskogo Pedinstituta* (*Transactions of the Murmansk Pedagogical College*), II (1958), 179-202

113
Spector, Robert D. "Attacks on the *Critical Review* in the *Court Magazine*" *Notes and Queries,* n.s. v (1958), 308

Lists six attacks on the *Critical Review* which appeared in the *Court Magazine* in 1761 and 1762.

114
Strauss, Albrecht B. "On Smollett's Language: a Paragraph in *Ferdinand Count Fathom*" *Style in Prose Fiction,* ed. Harold C. Martin New York: Columbia University Press, 1959 Pp. 25-54

Analyzes various aspects of Smollett's style including his diction, his use of figurative language, and his use of dialect and animal imagery to portray characters.

115
Warner, Oliver. *English Maritime Writing: Hakluyt to Cook* London: Longmans, 1958 Pp. 35

Briefly mentions Smollett's role in maritime writing – as a novelist and as an editor of "Collections" of travel literature. (See p. 26.)

1959

116
Batson, Eric J. and Stanley Weintraub "Eliza's Prototypes?" Letters in *Times Literary Supplement,* 13 November, p. 668

Batson and Weintraub note the influence of *Peregrine Pickle* on Shaw's *Pygmalion.* See also Albrecht B. Strauss, *Times Literary Supplement,* 11 December, p. 725.

117
Goldberg, Milton A. *Smollett and the Scottish School: Studies in Eighteenth-Century Thought*
Albuquerque: University of New Mexico Press, 1959 Pp. xiii + 191

Reviews
Sheridan Baker, *Modern Language Notes,* LXXV, 359-63
R. L. Brett, *Modern Language Review,* LV, 108-9
George Falle, *University of Toronto Quarterly,* XXX, 95-100
Byron Gassman, *Modern Philology,* LVII, 277-9
James Kinsley, *Review of English Studies,* n.s. XI, 335-6
John Lothian, *Aberdeen University Review,* XXXVIII, 261-2
C. J. Rawson, *Notes and Queries,* n.s. VI, 421-2
Ralph M. Williams, *College English,* XXI, 70

Traces a number of antithetical ideas in Smollett's novels (for example, primitivism and progress in *Humphry Clinker*) and points out Smollett's kinship to the Scottish Common-Sense School.

118
Orowitz, Milton "Craft and Vision in the Novels of Smollett: the Uses of Caricature" Dissertation, University of California, Berkeley, 1959

119
Roper, Derek "Smollett's 'Four Gentlemen': The First Contributors to the *Critical Review*" *Review of English Studies,* n.s. X (1959), 38-44

Identifies the "four gentlemen" who contributed to the first and second volumes of the *Critical Review* (1756) and lists the works which Smollett himself reviewed in these two volumes.

120
Spector, Robert D. "Smollett's Use of 'Tsonnonthouan'"
Notes and Queries, n.s. VI (1959), 112-13

Suggests that echoes of the *Memoirs of the Life and Adventures of Tsonnonthouan* appear in several of Smollett's works.

1960

121
Boggs, W. Arthur "Hassock of Hair" *Notes and Queries,* n.s. VII (1960), 72-3

A phrase used by Win Jenkins in *Humphry Clinker.*

122
Gassman, Byron Walter "The Background of *Humphry Clinker*" Dissertation, Chicago, 1960

Considers such matters as the personal, social, political, and religious backgrounds of *Humphry Clinker.*

123
Knapp, Lewis M. "Another Letter from Smollett to Dr. William Hunter" *Notes and Queries,* n.s. VII (1960), 299-300

124
McCombie, F. "*Count Fathom* and *El Buscón*" *Notes and Queries,* n.s. VII (1960), 297-9

Contends that Quevedo's *La Vida Del Buscón* influences *Ferdinand Count Fathom.*

125
Paulson, Ronald "Satire in the Early Novels of Smollett" *Journal of English and Germanic Philology,* LIX (1960), 381-402

Explores the relationship of formal verse satire, the picaresque, and the Jonsonian theory of humours to the satire in the early novels.

126
Sen, Sailendra K. "Sheridan's Literary Debt: *The Rivals* and *Humphry Clinker*" *Modern Language Quarterly,* XXI (1960), 291-300

127
Smollett, Tobias *The Expedition of Humphry Clinker* Foreword by Monroe Engel
New York: New American Library (Signet), 1960 Pp. 350

128
Spector, Robert D. "Attacks on the *Critical Review* in the *Literary Magazine*" *Notes and Queries,* n.s. VII (1960), 300-1

Cites three previously unrecorded attacks on the *Critical Review* which appeared in the *Literary Magazine* in 1757.

129
Spector, Robert D. "The *Monthly* and Its Rival" *Bulletin of the New York Public Library,* LXVI (1960), 159-61

Describes the effect of the *Critical Review* upon the older periodical.

1961

130
Baker, Sheridan "*Humphry Clinker* as Comic Romance" *Papers of the Michigan Academy of Science, Arts, and Letters,* XLVI (1961), 645-54

Discusses how Smollett in *Humphry Clinker* makes "romance assume the sock" through Lydia, Tabitha, and Clinker.

131
Boggs, W. Arthur "Win Jenkins' Malapropisms" *The Jammu and Kashmir University Review,* IV (1961), 130-40

132
Farrell, William Joseph "Rhetorical Elements in the Eighteenth-Century English Novel" Dissertation, Wisconsin, 1961 *Dissertation Abstracts,* XXII, 1976

Chapter IV (pp. 174-227) is devoted to Smollett.

133
Griffith, Philip M. "Fire-Scenes in Richardson's *Clarissa* and Smollett's *Humphry Clinker*: A Study of a Literary Relationship in the Structure of the Novel" *Tulane Studies in English*, XI (1961), 39-51

Asserts that in the two fire scenes in *Humphry Clinker* Smollett echoes and ridicules Richardson.

134
Lloyd, Christopher and Jack Coulter *Medicine and the Navy*, III Edinburgh: Livingstone, 1961 Pp. 25-8

Discusses a surgeon's mate's life aboard ship as Smollett depicted it in *Roderick Random.*

135
Wagoner, Mary H. S. "The Changing Patterns of Humor in the Novels of Tobias Smollett" Dissertation, Texas, 1961 *Dissertation Abstracts*, XXII, 1982

Traces "dual lines of development in Smollett's humor: the modifications in assumptions about society and its ills which underlie his laughter and the modifications in his techniques for generating laughter."

136
Webster, Grant "Smollett and Shaw: a Note on a Source for *Heartbreak House*" *Shaw Review*, IV (1961), 16-17

Points out the influence of *Peregrine Pickle* on Shaw's *Heartbreak House.*

1962

137
Aubrun, C. "Smollett et Cervantes" *Etudes Anglaises*, XV (1962), 122-9

138
Davis, Wendell Eugene "The World of Smollett's Novels: a Study of Travels and Setting" Dissertation, Western Reserve, 1962

Examines the sense of environment in Smollett's novels by discussing what influences his treatment of setting: drama and travel literature, the Gothic and the Picturesque.

139
Horn, András *Byron's "Don Juan" and the Eighteenth-Century English Novel* Bern: Francke, 1962 Pp. 75

Discusses picaresque elements in Byron's "Don Juan" and in Smollett's novels and concludes that Smollett influenced Byron. See Chapter III, pp. 49-60.

140
Lott, John Raymond "The Vogue of the Betrayed-Woman Theme in English Fiction, 1740-1775" Dissertation, Duke, 1962

Includes some discussion of this theme in Smollett's novels.

141
Marshall, Percy *Masters of the English Novel*
London: Dennis Dobson, 1962 Pp. 224

Chapter IV (pp. 60-75) is devoted to Smollett.

142
Maxwell, J. C. "French Borrowings in *Ferdinand Count Fathom*" *Notes and Queries,* n.s. IX (1962), 18-19

Lists three terms from *Ferdinand Count Fathom* which antedate the earliest use of these words recorded in the *Oxford English Dictionary.*

143
Mayo, Robert D. *The English Novel in the Magazines, 1740-1815*
Evanston: Northwestern University Press, 1962 Pp. x + 695

See pp. 274-88 especially, "Smollett and the *British Magazine*," which are concerned with *Sir Launcelot Greaves.*

144
Park, William John "The Mid-Eighteenth-Century English Novel" Dissertation, Columbia, 1962 *Dissertation Abstracts,* XXIV, 1163

A broad study of the mid-century novel with some discussion of Smollett.

145
Smollett, Tobias *Roderick Random* Introduction by Bergen Evans New York: Fawcett World Library (Premier), 1962 Pp. 446

1963

146
Alberts, Robert C. "The Fantastic Adventures of Captain Stobo" *American Heritage,* XIV (1963), 65-77

Conjectures that Stobo was a possible model for Lismahago, who appears in *Humphry Clinker.*

147
Al-Usaily, M. A. "Satire in the Novels of Smollett" Dissertation, Edinburgh, 1963

148
Baker, Sheridan "The Idea of Romance in the Eighteenth-Century Novel" *Studies in English Literature* (University of Tokyo), XXXIX (1963), 49-61

Smollett is mentioned on pp. 57-9.

149
Boggs, W. Arthur "Smollett's Coinages in the Win Jenkins' Letters" *Language Quarterly,* II (1963), 2-4

150
Gassman, Byron "The *Briton* and *Humphry Clinker*" *Studies in English Literature 1500-1900,* III (1963), 397-414

Examines the *Briton,* the *Complete History of England,* and the *Continuation of the Complete History* for Smollett's political views which reappear in *Humphry Clinker.*

151
Hannum, Howard L. "Tobias Smollett: Fiction and Caricature" Dissertation, University of Pennsylvania, 1963 *Dissertation Abstracts,* XXIV, 4189

Explores "the effects of painting and engraving – particularly of caricature – from the Renaissance to [Smollett's] own day upon his five novels." Emphasizes Hogarth's influence upon Smollett.

152
Hunting, Robert "Footnote to a Comparative Study: Smollett and Ibsen" *Notes and Queries,* n.s. X (1963), 228-9

Finds many parallels to Ibsen's *An Enemy of the People* in Smollett's "An Essay on the External Use of Water."

153
Knapp, Lewis M. and Lillian de la Torre "Smollett, MacKercher, and the Annesley Claimant" *English Language Notes,* I (1963), 28-33

Provides historical background for Smollett's account of the Annesley case, which appears in *Peregrine Pickle.*

154
Piper, William Bowman "The Large Diffused Picture of Life in Smollett's Early Novels" *Studies in Philology,* LX (1963), 45-56

Discusses characterization in Smollett's early novels.

155
Singer, Godfrey Frank *The Epistolary Novel: Its Origin, Development, Decline, and Residuary Influence*
New York: Russell and Russell, 1963 Pp. ix + 266

Briefly discusses *Humphry Clinker* as an epistolary novel.

156
Webster, Grant T. "The Novels of Tobias Smollett: A Study in Structures" Dissertation, Ohio State, 1963 *Dissertation Abstracts,* XXIV, 2914

Examines the comic-romantic plots of Smollett's novels from the standpoint of myth and analyzes the contrasting sentimental and satirical elements within the works.

157
Wilson, J. Stewart "Novel Into Play. The Influence of Richardson, Fielding, Smollett, and Sterne Upon the Later English Drama" Dissertation, Rice, 1963

1964

158
Alter, Robert B. *Rogue's Progress: Studies in the Picaresque Novel*
Cambridge, Massachusetts: Harvard University Press, 1964 Pp. xi + 148

Chapter IV, "The Picaroon as Fortune's Plaything," deals with *Roderick Random,* which derives from the continental picaresque novel, according to Alter. (Originally, this book was a dissertation – Harvard, 1962.)

159
Bache, Kaye E. "The Narrative Posture in Four Novels of Tobias Smollett" Dissertation, Wisconsin, 1964 *Dissertation Abstracts,* XXV, 2485

Investigates "what seems to be the basic structural determinant [of *Roderick Random, Peregrine Pickle, Ferdinand Count Fathom,* and *Humphry Clinker*], the narrative posture, and describes its biases, its rationale, and its diction."

160
Boggs, W. Arthur "A Win Jenkins' Lexicon" *Bulletin of the New York Public Library,* LXVIII (1964), 323-30

Defines most of Win's "strange, unfamiliar, or eighteenth-century usages," which may baffle the modern reader.

161
Bruce, Donald *Radical Doctor Smollett*
London: Gollancz, 1964 Pp. 240

Reviews
Roger Fulford, *Contemporary Review,* CCV, 663-4
V. S. Pritchett, *New Statesman,* LXVIII, 791-2
Times Literary Supplement, 31 December, p. 1182

Examines such diverse topics as the following: Smollett's reputation, his knowledge of medicine and determinist philosophy, his concept of love, his liberalism and social criticism, and the structure, style, and satiric techniques of his novels.

162
Jefferson, D. W. "Speculation on Three Eighteenth-Century Prose Writers" *Of Books and Humankind: Essays and Poems Presented to Bonomy Dobrée,* ed. John Butt
London: Routledge and Kegan Paul, 1964 Pp. 81-91

Discusses the "Augustan style" of *Ferdinand Count Fathom.*

163
Knapp, Lewis M. "The Keys to Smollett's *Atom*" *English Language Notes,* II (1964), 100-2

Provides a 1769 key to the characters and places which figure in the *Atom.*

164
Paulson, Ronald "Smollett and Hogarth: The Identity of Pallet" *Studies in English Literature 1500-1900,* IV (1964), 351-9

Maintains that Hogarth is the model for Pallett of *Peregrine Pickle.*

165
Preston, Thomas R. "Smollett and the Benevolent Misanthrope Type" *Publications of the Modern Language Association,* LXXIX (1964), 51-7

Traces Matt Bramble's literary antecedents.

166
Smollett, Tobias *Peregrine Pickle* Edited with an introduction by James L. Clifford
London: Oxford University Press, 1964 Pp. xxxiv + 805

Review
P. G. Boucé, *Etudes Anglaises,* XVIII, 196-7

167
Smollett, Tobias *Roderick Random* Afterword by John Barth
New York: New American Library (Signet), 1964 Pp. 479

168
Warner, John Maynard "Smollett and the Minor Comic Novel, 1750-1770" Dissertation, Harvard, 1964

1965

169
Boggs, W. Arthur "Dialectal Ingenuity in *Humphry Clinker*" *Papers on Language and Literature,* I (1965), 327-37

Examines words in Win Jenkins' letters drawn from several dialects – Welsh, London English, and Lowland Scotch.

170
Boggs, W. Arthur "Shakespeare and Win" *American Notes and Queries,* III (1965), 149-50

Shakespearian echoes in Win Jenkins' letters.

171
Boggs, W. Arthur "Some Standard Eighteenth-Century English Usages" *Quarterly Journal of Speech,* LI (1965), 304-6

Examines Win Jenkins' language.

172
Boggs, W. Arthur "Win Jenkins' Archaisms and Proverbial Phrases" *Language Quarterly,* IV (1965), 33-6

173
Boggs, W. Arthur "Win Jenkins' First Citations in the *Oxford English Dictionary*" *Word Study,* XLI (1965), 5

174
Boucé, Paul-Gabriel "Smollett's Libel" A letter in the *Times Literary Supplement,* 30 December, p. 1218

Concerns Smollett's libelous comments on Admiral Knowles in the *Critical Review.*

175
Elmer, Robert W. "Structure in the Early Novels of Smollett" Dissertation, Columbia, 1965 *Dissertation Abstracts,* XXVIII, 4123A

Refutes the idea that the novels are primarily satirical and contends that "they are organized by structures deriving principally from the melodramatic (taken in an entirely neutral sense), the comic, the values of sensibility, and, in one case especially, the presence of a distinctly conceived narrator." Concludes that "the novels also possess compatibility and unity of structure."

176
Gassman, Byron "Religious Attitudes in the World of Humphry Clinker" *Brigham Young University Studies,* VI (1965), 65-72

Argues that Smollett's view of religion in *Humphry Clinker* is basically satiric, especially in his treatment of Methodism.

177
Jennings, Edward Morton "Reader-Narrative Relationships in *Tom Jones, Tristram Shandy,* and *Humphry Clinker*" Dissertation, Wisconsin, 1965 *Dissertation Abstracts,* XXVI, 3303

Approaches these three novels "in terms of the reader's distance from and his involvement with the narrative" and discusses the significance of the multiple point of view and the epistolary mode used in *Humphry Clinker.*

178
Klukoff, Philip J. "A Smollett Attribution in the *Critical Review*" *Notes and Queries,* n.s. XII (1965), 221

Attributes to Smollett authorship of the editorial preface to Volume XI of the *Critical Review* for January 1761.

179
Klukoff, Philip J. "Smollett and the *Critical Review*: Criticism of the Novel" Dissertation, Michigan State, 1965 *Dissertation Abstracts,* XXVII, 748A

Investigates the extent of Smollett's influence on the criticism of the novel in the *Critical Review* and examines Smollett's (as well as the *Review*'s) concept of the novel as a genre.

180
Knapp, Lewis M. "Comments on Smollett by the Rev. Dr. Thomas Birch" *Notes and Queries,* n.s. XII (1965), 218-21

Reprints portions of letters written by Birch between 1746 and 1762 concerning Smollett and his work.

181
Knapp, Lewis M. "The 'Prophecy' attributed to Smollett" *Review of English Studies,* n.s. XVI (1965), 177-82

Conjectures that Smollett probably wrote the "Prophecy," but offers no conclusive data to support this view.

182
Knapp, Lewis M. "Smollett's Translation of Fénelon's *Télémaque*" *Philological Quarterly,* XLIV (1965), 405-7

Attributes this work to Smollett because of a document, dated 1767 and signed by Smollett, which Knapp supplies.

183
Reid, B. L. "Smollett's Healing Journey" *Virginia Quarterly Review,* XLI (1965), 549-70

Concerned with the changes (both physical and mental) which the characters undergo on their journey in *Humphry Clinker.*

1966

184
Bevis, Richard W. "Smollett and *The Israelites*" *Philological Quarterly,* XLV (1966), 387-94

Attributes "The Israelites," a farce performed in 1785, to Smollett.

185
Boggs, W. Arthur "'Birthday Suit' and 'Cheese-Toaster'" *Notes and Queries,* n.s. XIII (1966), 465

Discusses these terms, which appear in Smollett's novels.

186
Boggs, W. Arthur "Win Jenkins' Addenda to Mr. Murray's Dictionary" *Discourse,* IX (1966), 83-91

Examines the *Oxford English Dictionary*'s use of Win Jenkins' words and phrases.

187
Boucé, Paul-Gabriel "Les Procédés du comique dans *Humphry Clinker*" *Etudes Anglaises: Actes du Congrès de Lille,* XXV (1966), 53-75

Discusses the "cathartic humor" of *Humphry Clinker,* which distinguishes it from Smollett's other novels.

188
Elistratova, A. *Anglyisky Roman Epochy Prosvestchenia* (*The English Novel of the Enlightenment*)
Moscow: Nauka, 1966 Pp. 472

Review
L. Arinshtein, *Philological Quarterly,* XLVII, 329-31

See Chapters V and VIII, entitled "The Early Smollett" and "The Mature Smollett."

189
Fisher, Franklin F. "Smollett and the Premises of Fiction in the Eighteenth Century" Dissertation, University of California, Santa Barbara, 1966 *Dissertation Abstracts,* XXVIII, 1048A

Outlines Smollett's debt to Fielding as a novelist and "analyzes the structural dislocation that mars every novel after *Roderick Random* as a result of the author's inability to reconcile the representation of human experience with the premises of the [Fielding] convention."

190
Garrow, Scott "A Study of the Organization of Smollett's *The Expedition of Humphry Clinker*" *Southern Quarterly,* IV (1966), 349-63; V (1966), 22-46

Examines the Bramble party's itinerary and the novel's five subplots.

191
Klukoff, Philip J. "Smollett as the Reviewer of *Jeremiah Grant*" *Notes and Queries,* n.s. XIII (1966), 466

Attributes to Smollett a review of *Jeremiah Grant,* which appeared in the *Critical Review* of January 1763.

192
Klukoff, Philip J. "Smollett and the *Critical Review*: Criticism of the Novel, 1756-1763" *Studies in Scottish Literature,* IV (1966), 89-100

193
Klukoff, Philip J. "Two Smollett Attributions in the *Critical Review*: *The Reverie* and *Tristram Shandy*" *Notes and Queries,* n.s. XIII (1966), 465-6

194
Knapp, Lewis M. "Early Scottish Attitudes toward Tobias Smollett" *Philological Quarterly,* XLV (1966), 262-9

Describes the attitudes of various fellow Scots (such as the fifth Earl of Leven, Dr. Alexander Carlyle, and John Ramsay) towards Smollett.

195
Park, William "Fathers and Sons – *Humphry Clinker*" *Literature and Psychology,* XVI (1966), 166-74

A mythic-archetypal reading of *Humphry Clinker.*

196
Parreaux, André *Smollett's London: A Course of Lectures Delivered at the University of Paris, 1963-64*
Paris: Nizet, 1966 Pp. 189

Review
Times Literary Supplement, 27 April, p. 360

A historical study of eighteenth-century London with numerous references to the city as it appears in Smollett's works.

197
Rousseau, George S. "Doctors and Medicine in the Novels of Tobias Smollett" Dissertation, Princeton, 1966 *Dissertation Abstracts,* XXVII, 2160A

Shows "how the science of the day shaped the form and substance and tone of [Smollett's] fiction."

198
Shaw, James West "Caricature in the Novels of Tobias Smollett: Its Form and Function" Dissertation, Michigan, 1966 *Dissertation Abstracts,* XXVIII, 242A

Discusses Smollett's debt to the pictorial tradition for his caricature and observes that his novels exhibit a tendency to move from "caricature-portraits to character-portraits."

199
Smollett, Tobias *The Expedition of Humphry Clinker* Edited with an introduction by Lewis M. Knapp
London: Oxford University Press, 1966 Pp. xxii + 375

200
Wagoner, Mary "On the Satire in *Humphry Clinker*" *Papers on Language and Literature,* II (1966), 109-16

Argues that the satire of *Humphry Clinker* is influenced by Swift and Pope rather than by the picaresque writers.

1967

201
Bloch, Tuvia "Smollett's Quest for Form" *Modern Philology,* LXV (1967), 103-13

Contends that the form of *Humphry Clinker* was arrived at "through an effort to obviate the difficulties he had encountered" with the "Fielding type of novel" – *Ferdinand Count Fathom* and *Sir Launcelot Greaves.*

202
Boucé, Paul-Gabriel "The 'Chinese Pilot' and 'Sa-Rouf' in Smollett's *Atom*" *English Language Notes,* IV (1967), 273-5

Corrects errors of identification in an earlier key to the *Atom.*

203
Boucé, Paul-Gabriel "*Smollett Criticism, 1770-1924*: Corrections and Additions" *Notes and Queries,* n.s. XIV (1967), 184-7

Corrects and adds to Cordasco's bibliography of 1948.

204
Boucé, Paul-Gabriel "Smollett and the Expedition Against Rochefort (1757)" *Modern Philology,* LXV (1967), 33-8

Provides "historical and polemical background" for Smollett's attack upon Admiral Knowles.

205
Brack, O. M., Jr. "The Bicentennial Edition of the Works of Tobias Smollett" *Books at Iowa,* No. 7 (1967), 41-2

Describes the University of Iowa's edition of Smollett's works to appear in 1971.

206
Clements, Francis M. "Social Criticism in the English Novel: 1740-1754" Dissertation, Ohio State, 1967 *Dissertation Abstracts,* XXVIII, 5011A

Occasional references to social criticism in *Peregrine Pickle* and *Roderick Random.*

207
Driskell, Leon V. "Looking for Dustwich" *Texas Studies in Literature and Language,* IX (1967), 85-90

Concerns the first two letters in *Humphry Clinker.*

208
Evans, David L. "The Developing Satire of Smollett's Novels" Dissertation, University of Washington, 1967 *Dissertation Abstracts,* XXIX, 227A

Examines the kinds of satire in Smollett's prose fiction and the changes that this satire undergoes in the course of his career as a novelist.

209
Evans, David L. "*Humphry Clinker:* Smollett's Tempered Augustanism"
Criticism, IX (1967), 257-74

Examines the Augustan "myth of rural simplicity, retirement and order" as it appears in *Humphry Clinker.*

210
Giddings, Robert *The Tradition of Smollett*
London: Methuen, 1967 Pp. 215

Reviews
P. G. Boucé, *Etudes Anglaises,* XX, 312-13
Benjamin Boyce, *English Language Notes,* V, 63-5
André Parreaux, *Hermathena,* CV, 102-3
Juliet Sutton, *Dalhousie Review,* XLVII, 585-6
Times Literary Supplement, 29 June, p. 576

The "tradition" mentioned in the title is the picaresque tradition.

211
Grant, Damian J. "Unpublished Additions to Smollett's *Travels*"
Notes and Queries, n.s. XIV (1967), 187-9

Provides several of Smollett's additions and corrections to his own copy of the *Travels,* which Thomas Seccombe omitted in his 1907 edition of that work.

212
Iser, Wolfgang "Wirklichkeit und Form in Smolletts *Humphry Clinker*"
Europäische Aufklärung: H. Dieckmann zum 60 Geburtstag Hugo Friedrich and Fritz Schalk, eds.
Munich: Fink, 1967 Pp. 87-115

Discusses how a sense of verisimilitude is created by the form of *Humphry Clinker.*

213
Kent, John P. "Smollett's Translation of the *Gil Blas*: a Question of Text" *English Language Notes,* v (1967), 21-6

Asserts that Smollett bases his translation on the 1732-7 version of *Gil Blas.*

214
Klukoff, Philip J. "New Smollett Attributions in the *Critical Review*" *Notes and Queries,* n.s. xiv (1967), 418-19

Attributes to Smollett reviews of *Rasselas,* Adam Smith's *Theory of Moral Sentiments,* and Alexander Gerard's *Essay on Taste.*

215
Korte, Donald M. "Satire in Verse and in Prose: a Study of Smollett" Dissertation, Syracuse, 1967 *Dissertation Abstracts,* xxviii, 4602A

Explores the relationship between Smollett's "Advice" and "Reproof" (as well as other formal verse satires) and Smollett's novels.

216
Musher, Daniel M. "The Medical Views of Dr. Tobias Smollett (1721-1771)" *Bulletin of the History of Medicine,* xli (1967), 455-62

Reviews, explains, and assesses Smollett's medical views. Concludes that despite holding some mistaken opinions Smollett "observed perceptively and wrote brilliantly of factors important to man's physical and emotional health."

217
Paulson, Ronald *Satire and the Novel in Eighteenth-Century England* New Haven: Yale University Press, 1967 Pp. 318

Reviews
Frank Brady, *Studies in English Literature 1500-1900,* viii, 564-5
J. A. Rycenga, *Library Journal,* xcii, 3424
Yale Review, lvii, p. viii

See especially Chapter v, "Smollett: the Satirist as a Character Type," pp. 165-218 and portions of Chapter vi, "Satire and Sentimentality."

218
Rousseau, George S. "Matt Bramble and the Sulphur Controversy in the XVIIIth Century" *Journal of the History of Ideas,* XXVIII (1967), 577-89

Background on the medical satire in *Humphry Clinker.*

219
Rousseau, George S. "Smollett's *Acidum Vagum*" *Isis,* LVIII (1967), 244-5

Provides background on this chemical term which Ferret refers to in *Sir Launcelot Greaves.*

220
Smollett, Tobias "Advice" and "Reproof" Edited with an introduction by Donald M. Korte *Thoth,* VIII (1967), 45-65

In his notes to these verse satires the editor indicates numerous echoes of Pope and identifies individuals alluded to by Smollett.

221
Smollett, Tobias *The Expedition of Humphry Clinker* Edited with an introduction by Angus Ross
Harmondsworth: Penguin, 1967 Pp. 414

222
Stevick, Philip "Stylistic Energy in the Early Smollett" *Studies in Philology,* LXIV (1967), 712-19

Describes Smollett's energetic, often hyperbolic, mode of expression in the early novels.

223
Webster, Grant T. "Smollett's Microcosms: a Satiric Device in the Novel" *Satire Newsletter,* V (1967), 34-7

Discusses Smollett's use of the microcosm, which Webster defines as "a little world set within the plot of an episodic novel, in which a number of humor characters are presented and exposed as frauds."

1968

224
Battestin, Martin C. "On the Contemporary Reputations of *Pamela, Joseph Andrews,* and *Roderick Random*: Remarks by an 'Oxford Scholar,' 1748" *Notes and Queries,* n.s. xv (1968), 450-2

Prints some critical remarks on *Roderick Random,* from a pamphlet published in 1748.

225
Bloch, Tuvia "Smollett and the Jewish Naturalization Bill of 1753" *Notes and Queries,* vi (1968), 116-17

Finds no evidence in Smollett's depiction of Jews to support the claim that he was a humanitarian.

226
Duncan, Jeffrey L. "The Rural Ideal in Eighteenth-Century Fiction" *Studies in English Literature 1500-1900,* viii (1968), 517-35

See especially pp. 520-3 for a discussion of the rural ideal in *Humphry Clinker.*

227
Felsenstein, F. "A Note on Smollett's *Travels*" *Notes and Queries,* n.s. xv (1968), 452-3

Corrects the manuscript additions and corrections to Smollett's *Travels,* which Damian J. Grant cites in *Notes and Queries,* n.s. xiv (1967), 187-9

228
Goldknopf, Irma "Crime and Prison-Experience in the Early English Novel: Defoe, Fielding, Smollett" Dissertation, Syracuse, 1968 *Dissertation Abstracts,* xxix, 1207A

Explores "the reasons for the popularity of crime and imprisonment as subject matter for the novel and the literary exploitation of this subject matter" by Defoe, Fielding, and Smollett. Observes that Smollett "builds his satire on a realistic base to create an image of prison life as a microcosm of social existence."

229
Klukoff, Philip J. "Smollett and the Sackville Controversy" *Neuphilologische Mitteilungen,* LXIX (1968), 617-28

Attributes to Smollett various reviews (in the *Critical Review*) of pamphlets which attacked George Sackville, Lord Germain.

230
Knapp, Lewis M. "Smollett and Johnson, Never Cater-Cousins?" *Modern Philology,* LXVI (1968), 152-4

Considers the possibility that Johnson and Smollett were good friends.

231
Lindquist, Wayne Paul "Smollett and the Structure of the Novel" Dissertation, Iowa, 1968 *Dissertation Abstracts,* XXIX, 1872A

Maintains that "Smollett's plots were carefully planned and that he left the structure of the novel more mature, complex, and useful than he ever found it in his predecessors." Also assesses Smollett's debt to the picaresque tradition.

232
Rice, Scott Bradley "Smollett's *Travels Through France and Italy* and the Genre of Grand Tour Literature" Dissertation, Arizona, 1968 *Dissertation Abstracts,* XXIX, 2682A

Outlines the origins and salient features of the genre of Grand Tour literature and studies Smollett's *Travels* as an example of this genre.

233
Rosenmeier, Henrik "Tobias Smollett: A Study in Popular Taste at Mid-Century" Dissertation, Minnesota, 1968 *Dissertation Abstracts,* XXIX, 1905A

Primarily concerned with Smollett's novels, but also with the relationship of Smollett's *History of England* and the *Continuation* to the novels.

234
Roth, Barry "Smollett's Grub Street: a Study of the Development of an Artist" Dissertation, Stanford, 1968 *Dissertation Abstracts,* XXIX, 3981A

Examines Smollett's changing conception and treatment of Grub Street in his poetry and in his fiction.

235
Sena, John F. "Smollett's Persona and the Melancholic Traveler" *Eighteenth Century Studies,* I (1968), 353-69

Concerned with Smollett's *Travels Through France and Italy.*

236
Short, John D. "Smollett V. Armstrong: an Ascription of 'The Tears of Scotland' by Dr. Charles Burney" *Notes and Queries,* n.s. XV (1968), 453-6

Examines the case for Armstrong writing "The Tears of Scotland."

237
Skinner, Mary L. "The Interpolated Story in Selected Novels of Fielding and Smollett" Dissertation, Tennessee, 1968 *Dissertation Abstracts,* XXIX, 4020A

Concentrates upon "the form and function of interpolation in the works of Fielding and Smollett and their immediate antecedents." Concludes that the interpolated tales in Fielding and Smollett are "vitally organic parts of the works in which they appear." (Chapter III is devoted to Smollett's use of interpolation in *Roderick Random, Peregrine Pickle,* and *Humphry Clinker.*)

238
Smollett, Tobias "*The Adventures of Roderick Random.* A Critical Edition " Edited with an introduction by James Boyd Davis Dissertation, Virginia, 1968

Based on the first edition of *Roderick Random* and the revised editions of 1748, 1750, and 1755. In his introduction Davis shows how the values of the novel are inconsistent with those intended and with those avowed by the author.

239
Smollett, Tobias *The Expedition of Humphry Clinker* Edited with an introduction by André Parreaux
Boston: Houghton Mifflin (Riverside), 1968 Pp. xxxvii + 346

240
Spector, Robert D. *Tobias Smollett*
New York: Twayne, 1968 Pp. 175

A study of Smollett's literary achievement - especially his five novels, which are picaresque in form, according to Spector. Contains a chronology and a selected bibliography.

241
Wolf, J. Harry "Tobias Smollett and *The Orientalist*" *Notes and Queries,* n.s. xv (1968), 456-63

Conjectures that Smollett may have contributed to *The Orientalist,* but draws no conclusions.

Index

Index